A Leg to Stand On

Lois Olson

WestBow Press books may be ordered through booksellers or by contacting:

WestBow Press
A Division of Thomas Nelson & Zondervan
1663 Liberty Drive
Bloomington, IN 47403
www.westbowpress.com
1 (866) 928-1240

Because of the dynamic nature of the Internet, any web addresses or links contained in this book may have changed since publication and may no longer be valid. The views expressed in this work are solely those of the author and do not necessarily reflect the views of the publisher, and the publisher hereby disclaims any responsibility for them.

Any people depicted in stock imagery provided by Thinkstock are models, and such images are being used for illustrative purposes only. Certain stock imagery © Thinkstock.

ISBN: 978-1-4908-4833-4 (sc)
ISBN: 978-1-4908-4834-1 (e)

Library of Congress Control Number: 2014915091

Printed in the United States of America.

WestBow Press rev. date: 10/30/2014

WESTBOW·
PRESS
A DIVISION OF THOMAS NELSON
& ZONDERVAN

Dedicated to the Children of Cook Family Farm.......and Kip

Kip sounds off with three or four barks as my vehicle slowly drives up the long driveway to the house and out-buildings. He hops along the cars in a rocking horse motion. As a pup he lost his leg when he was hit by a car.

I am routinely greeted by this dog the same way whenever I go to visit the farm. Once Kip announces the visitors, he finds something else to do. He isn't one for petting and fussing over. So, we have agreed to our indifferences over these past years. I really don't believe I've ever petted him more than a couple of times, and he is content with that.

Kip and I have something in common. I don't think he knows this. He's a dog, after all. He's a big, brown, rough coated pooch of no particular breed. I watch him get around on his three strong legs and I respect him. Two years ago, I lost a leg by amputation.

Will I ever be as strong as Kip? I wonder. He doesn't need a prosthetic leg. I do.

On this particular day Kip made his usual announcement. Then I was greeted in the driveway by a half dozen excited children who were sweaty and dusty from playing on a hot summer day. Their hands and faces were all sticky from their last popsicles.

"Lois! Come and see Myrtle! She broke her leg!" As they all ran ahead to find the patient, I followed slowly back to the barn area.

"Can you do something to help her?", voices nervously asked.

Each bright eyed youngster watched as I evaluated Myrtle's leg. Acting like a true goat, this Saanen yearling had probably made a bad landing from a large wooden spool that had once been used for telephone wire. Now the goats used the spool for playground equipment.

And yes, her left front leg was fractured just above the knee.

Myrtle is 6 year old Ashley's 4H Club goat. Myrtle had won a coveted blue ribbon at last year's county fair. This injured animal was suddenly more important than the other chores on the farm that day.

Now Myrtle stood quietly, holding her leg to prevent further pain.

I sent some of the children back to the house to gather items needed to fashion a splint. Ashley held firmly onto Myrtle's collar while Austin, half her age, fired questions non-stop.

"Can you fix her leg?", Austin asked apprehensively.

"Yes, we are going to try to fix it."

"Does it hurt Myrtle?" And expression of compassion appeared on his face.

"I think so. She is being a very good goat, don't you think?"

"Can I help?"

"I'll let you hold something for me while I fix her leg." I suggested.

He beamed with pride at the thought of being my assistant.

The field became our treatment area. With the medical supplies, lots of helpers, and one rather confused goat, the project began. I spotted an old, cast-off tractor seat to use as a bench. Then I handed Austin the pink bandage wrap to hold until I was ready for it. He held it carefully with a serious look on his face.

Now came the task of forming a splint.

The children crowded in for a better view. The mosquitoes began dive-bombing and Myrtle nervously nibbled at my hair and earrings. Sweat dribbled down my forehead into my eyes making it difficult to see what I was doing.

On top of all these distractions, my prosthetic leg was refusing to stay attached while I wiggled around working on the splint. The children's eyes grew huge when I grabbed my leg and casually tossed it over by the fence.

Actually they knew I had a "fake leg" but they had never seen it as a separate entity.

Once I was free to move without the hassle of my leg, I began to assemble the splint. First, I wrapped the goat's leg with cotton batting. Then I broke a yard stick in half and placed one half on each side of the leg. I wrapped a pink stretchy bandage several times around the cotton batting and yardsticks.

Myrtle nervously nibbled at the loose ends of the bandage. I took the ends from her mouth and secured the wrap with a large safety pin. It was amazing how Myrtle stood completely still for the entire process. She must have known that we were helping her.

We all watched as Myrtle tried out her splinted leg. She took a few steps and then squatted to pee. At that we decided the job was a success. Ashley was again in hopes of earning another blue ribbon at the county fair this year.

A couple of the children returned the first-aid kit to the house while the others took Myrtle to her new stall to rest from others in the goat herd. Appreciating the quiet for a few moments, I began to think about the day ahead of me. I had originally come to help the family with their usual Tuesday chores and those still needed to be done.

It was clumsy reaching for my prosthesis, which was a bit farther away than I could easily reach. In moments like this I become frustrated. It truly was an inconvenience to deal with a prosthesis, especially when a prize winning 4-H goat belonging to a six-year-old girl seemed so much more important.

I scooted over to the leg and retrieved it. I began to put it on, sighing heavily. Suddenly I became distracted by the rocking- horse movement from the corner of my eye. As I sat there, still feeling a bit disheartened, Kip joined me.

Slowly, in total empathy, this very large, brown dog laid his head gently in my lap.

Those deep, soft eyes spoke to me. Through them Kip said, "It's OK. I understand. So does Myrtle."

Kip, the dog that never needed to be petted, was comforting me. Tears of appreciation ran down my face and our hearts met.

Soon the dusty, giggling children reappeared. Kip turned his attention to his charges. After all, the job of protecting and chaperoning the children was his responsibility.

But, for those few moments in the quiet, that old, lame dog with three legs protected me. Protected me from the discouragement he had already conquered.

CPSIA information can be obtained at www.ICGtesting.com
Printed in the USA
LVOW02s0810010615

440665LV00028B/499/P